G·E·T B·U·S·H·W·I·S·E

A BUSHVELD SAFARI

A Young Explorer's Guide to the Bushveld

D0573258

Nadine Clarke

DEDICATION

*To my children Ryan and Skye, and to
every other child around the world who
shares the awesome responsibility of
caring for our precious planet.*

Struik Publishers
(A division of New Holland Publishing (South Africa) (Pty) Ltd)
Cornelis Struik House
80 McKenzie Street
Cape Town 8001

New Holland Publishing is a member of the Johnnic Publishing Group.

www.struik.co.za

Log on to our photographic website
www.imagesofafrica.co.za for an African experience.

First published 2002
1 3 5 7 9 10 8 6 4 2

Copyright © in text: Nadine Clarke 2002
Copyright © in photographs: Nadine Clarke 2002;
individual photographers listed on p 63
Copyright © in published edition: Struik Publishers 2002

Publishing manager: Pippa Parker
Managing editor: Helen de Villiers
Editor: Katharina von Gerhardt
Designer: TLC Design
Illustrator: Jesse Breytenbach

Reproduction by Hirt and Carter Cape (Pty) Ltd
Printed and bound by Craft Print, Singapore

All rights reserved. No part of this publication may be reproduced, stored
in a retrieval system, or transmitted, in any form or by any means,
electronic, mechanical, photocopying, recording or otherwise, without
the prior written permission of the copyright owners and publishers.

ISBN 1 86872 736 X

CONTENTS

FOREWORD

A long time ago, I heard it said: 'The environment is like a village common — we all use it, but few take care of it.' More than two decades later, and in spite of growing interest in, and concern about the environment, these words still ring true.

In 1981, I opened the Lapalala Wilderness Environmental School in the Waterberg Mountains with the intention of awakening young people's minds to the value of caring for our world. Thousands of young people and teachers have since experienced and benefited from that outdoor classroom. One of the teachers participating at the school was Nadine Clarke. Nadine has now written her first book, entitled *A Bushveld Safari,* which will form part of a series of safari books. The idea for her book was conceived, I feel sure, as a result of her earlier experience of imparting knowledge of the bushveld to young enthusiasts.

A journey, any journey, begins with the first step, and this book will certainly be a first step for countless young readers in learning about the natural world — and why it is so important for us to care for it.

It is a great pleasure for me to write this foreword for Nadine, and I draw no small delight in having helped spark an interest in one generation of environmentalists, which is now being passed on to successive generations.

Clive H Walker

Jabu

INTRODUCTION

Imagine a place where toothbrushes are found in the wild, beans jump and snails' shells are as big as teacups; where the patterns in the sand tell amazing stories; where the garbage collectors are so small that they are easy to miss; where caterpillars walk in single file, and where birds guide you to delicious stores of honey. It sounds like a fantasy world, doesn't it? This place is called the Bushveld. In the course of this book, you are going to go on a walking safari through the Bushveld and you will see all these natural wonders, and more. Guiding you on this wonderful journey will be Jabu, who has lived in this wilderness all his life and discovered its secrets – many of which he will share with you.

My name is Jabu. I come from an ancient African people called the Shangaans. My father and grandfather were among the last remaining hunter-gatherers here in the wilderness. They hunted for meat and gathered food and medicine from the bush, but they never took more than they needed. They lived in harmony with the wild and gained a deep understanding of their environment. This knowledge has been passed on to me, and I am going to use it to take you on a journey of discovery.

'Bushveld' is the name we give the area, along with its associated animals, that runs through many of South Africa's game parks. The largest and most important of these is the Kruger National Park. The 'Big Five' - lion, leopard, buffalo, elephant and rhino - are found here. They are called the 'Big Five' because they are considered to be among the most dangerous animals to hunt. But don't be afraid. As long as you follow the **Get Bushwise** rules, you'll be fine.

AFRICA

Kruger Park

South Africa

THE *GET BUSHWISE* RULES ARE:

- Always walk in single file behind your guide.
- Never run, no matter how much you might want to.
- Obey your guide's hand signals at all times. Some of these are 'stop', 'come', 'crouch down' and 'listen'.
- Freeze as soon as your guide gives the 'stop' command.
- Don't touch anything strange, and don't eat anything out of the bush unless your guide tells you that it is safe.
- Don't damage any plants or frighten or injure any animals.
- Most importantly, remember that the wilderness is to be respected at all times.

Keep an eye out for **BB**, the Bushwise Beetle who leaves **'Did you know . . .?'** facts throughout the book. BB is a dung beetle. Just as she collects dung and gathers it into a ball in which to lay her precious eggs, so you can collect all the information in this book of discovery and use it wisely.

Some chapters feature **Activities**, which are fun things that you can try at home.

When you see words shown in **bold letters**, you can find out what these words mean by looking in the glossary on page 64.

Let's go and **GET BUSHWISE**!

As the sun rises in the east, we set off from our tented camp, walking in single file. Although it can get hot later in the day, it is still a little chilly this early in the morning. The air is heavy with the sweet scent of acacia blossoms. A chorus of birds sings us on our way. We venture into a wilderness that at first appears a little hostile and strange - we find it hard to imagine how early humans managed to survive in a place so foreign and wild. But nature is unkind only to those who do not try to understand it. For those who take the time to look a little closer, the Bushveld is a treasure chest filled with useful and beautiful surprises.

Emperor moth

THE BUSH SUPERMARKET

FUN IN THE SUN
We all know that the sun's scorching rays can damage our skin – but you don't need a sunblock cream to protect yourself from sunburn out here in the Bushveld. Follow the example of the wise and wrinkled elephant. Elephants love mud-bathing because, although their skin looks tough, it can also get sunburnt. Find some wet, fresh mud, and then plaster it all over your face and any other exposed parts of your body. The mud will protect you from the sun's dangerous rays, and also from stinging and biting insects. You might look a little odd, but the animals won't mind.

HUNGRY? GRUB'S UP!

Find a mopane tree and search its leaves for the scrumptious worms that feed on it in summer. These worms are the **larvae** of the emperor moth, and are high in protein, so they make a very nutritious snack. Try them either freshly picked from a mopane leaf, sun dried or in a stew. The first mouthful is always easier with your eyes closed!

Mopane worm

Magic guarri branch

THE TOOTHBRUSH TREE

If you are one of those people who brushes your teeth twice a day, it is time to find a magic guarri tree – a tree that occurs commonly in these parts. Cut off a small branch, remove the bark around the end, and then chew the end of the branch until the fibres become soft and resemble the head of a tooth-brush. Now you can brush and polish your teeth!

Acacia flowers

NATURE'S CUP

Look for an empty giant land snail shell and clean it out thoroughly. Then fill it with fresh water from your water bottle and wash down your mopane worm snack.

TOOTHPICK TRICK

Got a bit of mopane worm stuck between your teeth? Look for a sweet thorn tree, which belongs to the acacia family and is one of the most widespread trees in Africa. It has white thorns that can reach a length of seven centimetres – a very useful size for a toothpick. The gum of the tree, which oozes from its trunk, is edible, and can also be used as glue.

Giant land snail shell

Acacia branch

NOW FOR THE TOOTHPASTE

Leadwood makes excellent firewood, as it burns for a long time. When the fire's gone out, you can use the remaining ash as toothpaste.

HANDY HYGIENE

For a good, soapy hand wash, pick some leaves from the devil's thorn plant, add a little water, and rub them between your hands. The result is a wonderful frothy lather that can be used as soap or shampoo. This practical little plant can be found growing along the ground.

Baboon's tail plant

ALL TIED UP

The bark of the silver terminalia tree is very stringy and a few strips woven together can be used to make a strong, sturdy rope.

NIGHT FRIGHTS?

If you find yourself without a torch, search for a baboon's tail plant, which gets its name from its shape, and has fire-resistant black scales around the main part of the plant. Cut off the baboon's tail plant at ground level, remove the leaves, and dip the stem into any leftover cooking fat or lard. Then set it alight. It will burn for a long time, making a bright lamp.

DUNG DEFENCE

The elephant comes to our rescue yet again as the sun goes down and the mosquitoes start biting. Collect some elephant dung and burn it from time to time around the campsite – the smouldering dung helps to keep these little night-biters at bay.

NATURE NOTES

The bark of the paperbark tree peels off in large layers and makes useful sheets of paper. You have to write on it carefully, though, with a soft pencil, as it is quite brittle and tears very easily.

Silver terminalia branch

Porcupine quills

QUILL THRILL

Need a pen? A porcupine quill dipped in ink will do the trick. Be sure that the quill you find isn't still attached to a porcupine!

LEAFY LOO ROLL

When you need to go to the toilet in the Bushveld, you have to act a bit like a cat – dig a hole. A thick bunch of the soft leaves from the weeping wattle tree makes fine toilet paper.

LAUGH AT LARVAE

Want a giggle? Go and sit under a tamboti tree and watch its fallen beans jump. The seeds of this tree are often infested with the **larvae** of the jumping bean moth, and once the seeds have fallen from the tree, the wriggling **larvae** inside the seeds can cause the seeds to leap about.

Weeping wattle branch

Paperbark

DID YOU KNOW ...?

Hippos make their own sunblock

Hippos protect their sensitive skins from the harmful rays of the sun by secreting a thick, reddish fluid. They also avoid sunburn by remaining submerged in the water during the heat of the day.

The sun is climbing in the sky as we make our way towards the river. The bush music has changed from morning birdsong to the incessant humming of insects. One of the reasons hunter-gatherers like my Shangaan forefathers were able to survive in the Bushveld was that they learnt how to read nature's signs. Animal tracks are among these signs, and each footprint tells its own unique story: which kinds of animals were here, how many there were, what they were doing and in which direction they were going. Remember that a long time ago, following tracks to the actual animal determined whether or not supper would be served that night!

In order to work out what spoor belongs to which animal, and to interpret the silent story behind each footprint, we need to become Bushveld detectives. Some tracks, such as the elephant's, are enormous and easy to see, while others, such as the antlion's, are so tiny that we need a magnifying glass to examine them. Let's take a closer look!

KEEPING TRACK

STRANGE SIGNS

VERVET MONKEY

Much like a human's track: its front paw leaves a handprint and its back paw leaves a footprint. When the monkey sits and feeds, its tail rests on the ground, and this can look like a fifth 'footprint'.

(All animal tracks featured here are of the front foot and are LIFE SIZE!)

Vervet monkey

TORTOISE
A railway track. Tortoises walk on the tips of their heavily clawed feet, and move with their feet far apart, which is why their spoor looks like a railway track.

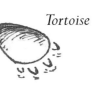

Tortoise

HELMETED GUINEAFOWL
A small bird footprint with definite claw marks and a clearly visible back-toe print. Francolins and partridges leave a similar print, but the Helmeted Guineafowl's footprint is quite large.

Guineafowl

SNAKE
A wavy line. It is not really possible to work out exactly what type of snake makes the line, as most Bushveld snakes leave this kind of trail.

Snake

ANTLION
A tiny pin-prick track. The inventive **larva** of the antlion digs a little pit, then climbs into it and waits hungrily at the bottom in the hope that an unwary ant will fall in. This clever creature excavates its pit at night, leaving a meandering trail of tracks that resemble pin-pricks across the sandy surface. If an animal track has these tiny trails across it, then we can deduce, as bushwise detectives, that the animal passed here *before* the antlion excavated its pit for the night.

Antlion

Making Tracks

Signs don't only occur in the wild — you can find them in your garden. Search for prints that cats, dogs and birds leave behind. Try to work out what they were doing and in which direction they went. How about making your own collection of them? This is easiest when the tracks are imprinted in dried mud.

WHAT YOU'LL NEED:
500 g bag of Plaster of Paris (available at your local pharmacy)
1 paper cup
1 litre (or 4 cups) water

WHAT TO DO:
1. Half-fill a paper cup with Plaster of Paris powder.
2. Slowly add water to the powder, stirring it all the while with a pencil or a stick. Keep adding water until the Plaster of Paris has the consistency of toothpaste — sticky but not firm.
3. Tap the cup on the ground six or seven times to ensure that all the air bubbles trapped in the Plaster of Paris are removed.
4. Before the plaster sets, pour it into the animal track until it flows over the sides of the footprint.
5. Wait about 30 minutes for the Plaster of Paris to harden.
6. Use a blunt knife to dig around the set Plaster of Paris, removing it from the mud.
7. Wash off the mud. You will see a copy of the track preserved in the Plaster of Paris.
8. Label the cast with the name of the animal and where and when it was found.

The base of your cast will resemble the underfoot of the animal.

Spotted hyaena

Lion

PAWS WITH CLAWS

SPOTTED HYAENA

Two lobes at the rear of the pad, and claw marks.
This track looks like a large dog's footprint, but the hindfoot
is smaller than the forefoot, because the hyaena is heavier
towards the front of its body.

LION

**Large pug marks without any visible claw
marks.** Most cats have three lobes at the rear
of the pad. You can't see claw marks in the
print as lions' claws are **retractable**.

Burchell's zebra

TRAILS THAT TROT

BURCHELL'S ZEBRA

A horseshoe. Zebras leave prints that look
very much like a horse's track.

IMPALA

**A short, neat, pointed track
that looks like an arrowhead.**
This buck walks on the tips
of its third and fourth
toes. The point of the
'arrowhead'
indicates the
direction in which
the animal was walking.

Impala

CIRCLES IN THE SAND

WHITE RHINO

An oval print with lobes. The 'W' at the rear of this track tells us this is a white rhino's track – 'W' for 'white'! (The black rhino's print has a slight curve at the rear of the print.)

ELEPHANT

A huge circular print. It can be up to 50 cm across, filled with criss-crossing cracks and furrows. Elephants have a thick layer of **cartilage** under their feet, which acts as a shock absorber to cushion their weight and enables them to walk through the Bushveld without making a sound.

White rhino

DID YOU KNOW...?

The ostrich leaves a unique track. It is the only African bird that leaves a two-toed track – because its foot is made up of just two toes! (This print is not its actual size, it's about a quarter of the true size.)

This elephant print is that of a teenager!!

Ostrich

TEST YOUR SKILLS

Trackers in action

1. How many impala came down for a drink at the waterhole?
2. Did they all leave the waterhole?
3. What do you think happened?
4. Did the zebra have a drink?
5. Was somebody following the zebra?
6. What did the rhino do?
7. Which tracks are not fresh?
8. How do you know this?
9. Which animal walked in a northerly direction?
   Use the compass rose (which shows north) to work this out.
10. Can you find the short monkey trail?
11. Where was the guineafowl?

* Answers on page 63.

N

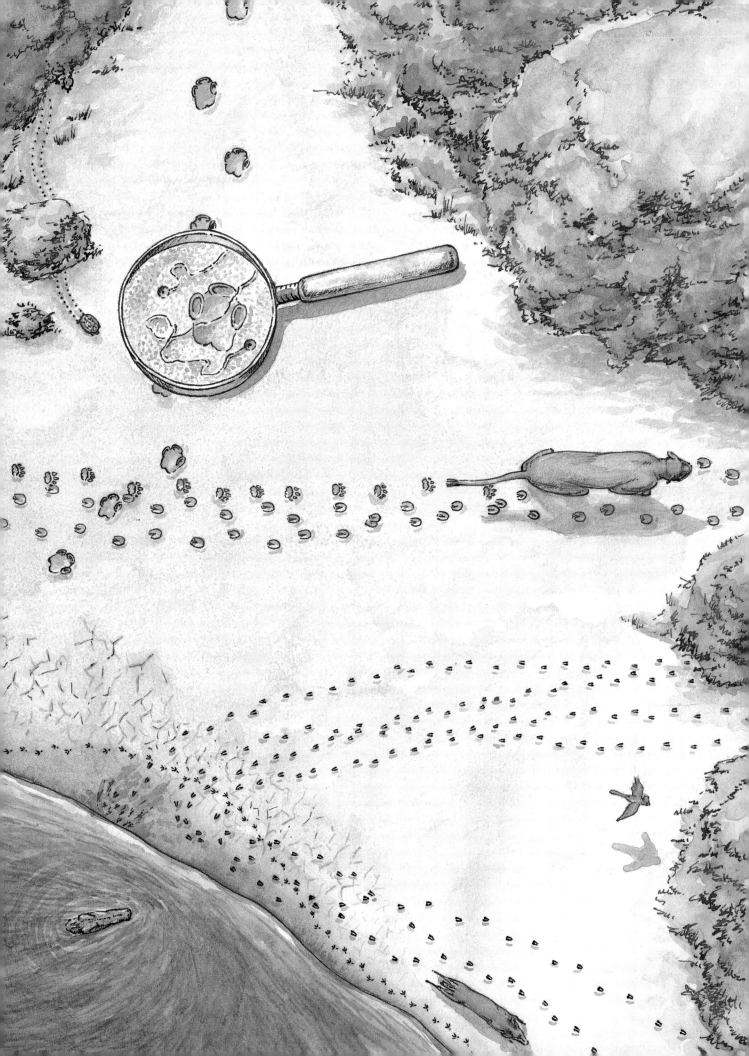

We follow a well-trodden path leading away from the river, which bears the tracks of all kinds of animals. Many generations of hippo and elephant families use the same path year after year. Suddenly, we come upon a clearing in the bush. There is a sharp cracking sound of splintering branches - and then we see them: a large herd of elephants, feeding off the nearby trees! Shhhh . . . we must be careful!

The first thing I am going to do is a 'wind test' so I can check whether the elephants can smell us or not. I pick up a handful of sand and, holding it quite far above the ground, let it trickle out between my fingers. The sand grains blow a little in our direction. This is good news, as it means we are **downwind** of the herd, so they can't pick up our scent. Keeping very quiet, we crouch down near a clump of bushes and scan the surroundings with our binoculars. If we look carefully, we can spot many **herbivores** feeding at different levels.

A MULTI-STOREY RESTAURANT

THE NEATENER
Burchell's zebra provide an all-round clear-up of untidy grasses. They enjoy feeding on sprouting grasses, but will also eat longer grass. They have strong, sensitive upper lips, which are used to push the greenery between their incisor teeth. The incisors are then used to cut the grass free.

Warthog

THE GARDENER

The warty warthog is perfectly equipped to find its particular kind of food: it has strong tusks with which to dig, a shovel-shaped nose for rooting about in the soil and tough, horny pads to protect its knobbly knees – which is just as well, as it spends a lot of its time kneeling down, uprooting **rhizomes** and bulbs with its tusks. When the warthog digs up the rhizomes, it **aerates** the soil and creates the necessary conditions for seeds to **germinate**. Warthogs also enjoy eating the fresh green shoots of grass.

Warthog tusk

THE LAWNMOWER

Want your grass cropped? Call in a white rhino! White rhinos have very wide, hard mouths that are perfectly suited to mowing lawns. These animals are called **grazers**. White rhinos eat very fast – up to 78 bites a minute, which is more than a mouthful a second! Next time your mother asks you not to gobble your food, you can tell her this.

THE HEDGE-CUTTER

If you require your garden shrubbery neatened up, then you need the black rhino. The black rhino is a **browser** – it picks leaves from trees and bushes using its special top lip, which folds into a hook. Another name for this rhino is 'hook-lipped rhino'. The black rhino is an **endangered** species because it is **poached** for its horn. Its horn is not special – it is made of **keratin**, which is the same substance that makes up our fingernails – but some people believe the horn can cure illnesses. This is nonsense, of course.

White rhino

Black rhino

THE CLEARER

The burly buffalo is able to digest long, **fibrous** grass. By moving through areas of old grass and grazing it, these animals open up areas, allowing new grass to grow.

African buffalo

THE TREE-TRIMMER
Have you got bushy trees? Then call in a kudu. Because of its size, the kudu **browses** higher than the black rhino, but lower than the giraffe.

Kudu

THE LADDER
Need work done right at the top of the tallest trees? The giraffe, with its long neck, is able to **browse** at heights of up to five metres, which is more than three times your height. Its favourite food is the leaves from the thorny acacia tree. Its long, leathery tongue, which can reach a length of 60 cm (that's two school rulers!), strips the leaves off the branches.

THE CLEANER-UPPER AND KNOCKER-DOWNER
Elephants can eat up to 170 kg of food a day (that's probably more than five times your body weight!), and are specially designed to make the most of everything that is available.

Elephants use their tusks and twirly trunks to get to their food. The tusks are used for digging up edible roots and for stripping bark from trees. Just as we are right- or left-handed, so too is the elephant right- or left-tusked: one tusk is always longer than the other. The short tusk is known as the 'slave tusk' and does all the work, while the longer one is called the 'master'.

The elephant uses its trunk to **browse** at all heights, from trees to grass, wrapping it around whatever juicy morsel it wants to eat. These gigantic **mammals** often push over trees while they are **browsing**. In this way, they provide food for **browsers** that wouldn't normally be able to reach the highest leaves, and they open up areas so that new grass can grow for **grazers**.

Giraffe

African elephant

THE ALL-ROUNDER
The impala is an adaptable feeder and will eat grass and the lower leaves from trees and bushes, as well as fruit and pods.

Impala

THE BAROMETER

Blue wildebeest are very sensitive to rain – they can hear and see it falling from up to 25 kilometres away! When they do, they immediately depart in search of those wetter, greener pastures. The blue wildebeest's favourite dish is the lower sections of grass, usually the fresh shoots that sprout after rain, and the young seedlings that pop up after veld fires. Blue wildebeest, which are **nomadic**, have a wide snout that enables them to crop the grass.

Blue wildebeest

TEST YOUR SKILLS

Who's eating what?

Grazers are animals that eat grass, while **browsers** are animals that eat leaves. Can you match the correct animal with the correct feeding level? The body parts below should give you a clue.

* Answers on page 63.

A

E

D

C

B

1

2

3

4

5

DID YOU KNOW...?

The giraffe has the same number of neck bones as you and me.

The giraffe is the tallest animal, so you'd expect it to have lots of extra bones in its neck, wouldn't you? But it doesn't. It has seven neck **vertebrae**, just as you do – and just as the smallest mouse does!

The elephants slowly meander off into dense bush, leaving behind torn branches, trampled grass and some massive piles of dung. Like enormous recycling machines rumbling through the bush, devouring bark, twigs and leaves, elephants can produce up to 100 kg of dung a day! Their dung *fertilizes* the soil, and plant seeds that have passed through the elephant's *intestine* are found in the dung, which provides them with ideal *germinating* conditions.

Suddenly, as if a school bell signal had gone out on the bush network, countless beetles come swarming in from all directions, landing on the dung. Beetles start energetically rolling balls of dung away in the strangest of ways – by standing on their forelegs with their heads down, pushing the dung balls with their hind legs. Now and again the beetles stop and clamber up on to their hard-won ball to have a better view of where they are going. These dung beetles, along with many other animals like hyaenas, millipedes and vultures, are the Bushveld's garbage collectors.

GARBAGE COLLECTORS

THE GARBAGE REMOVERS

The dutiful dung beetles are always on the lookout for a fresh pile of dung. Some dung beetles feed off dung, while others eat **carrion**, **fungus** or even leaf litter.

Dung beetles selecting their balls of dung

Certain **species** of dung beetle roll the dung into a ball with their spoon-shaped front legs. Once it has made its ball, the dung beetle lays its eggs in the dung ball. It then buries the ball containing the precious eggs underground, in order to maintain moisture and to protect the **larvae** from **predators**. When the **larvae** hatch, they munch away at the delicious dung for a few weeks.

The honey badger, a cunning thief, may at times destroy the dung beetle's future plans by digging up the ball and eating the **larvae** inside!

Dung beetle burying a dung ball

Cape Vulture

THE GARBAGE RECYCLERS

Scavengers very seldom hunt animals for food. They prefer to snatch a kill from lions or other **predators.** They also feed on what's left behind after the **predators** have eaten their fill at a kill.

VULTURE CULTURE

Vultures can spot a **carcass** from miles away. They are specialist **scavengers**, which means they only eat **carrion**.

BIG BULLY

The Lappet-faced Vulture is a very big bird – it has a wingspan of nearly three metres and its outstretched foot is the same size as a man's outstretched hand. Its bill is the largest of any bird of prey and can tear through the toughest skin. It's also very bad-tempered – one Lappet-faced Vulture can chase away 30 other **scavenging** birds!

GREEDY GOBBLER

The Cape Vulture can swallow a kilogram of food (that's about five hamburgers) in three minutes. Its tongue is the secret to its speed at the dinner table: it is grooved and serrated, which helps it to swallow quickly. The Cape Vulture inserts its head into the **carcass** and gobbles down the flesh and **intestines**.

FEEDING FRENZY

White-backed Vultures are real party animals – 200 of them can end up feeding at the same **carcass**! They tear through the softer skin of the belly of the dead animal and gorge themselves on the tasty **entrails**.

Lappet-faced Vulture

Black-backed jackal (above left) and spotted hyaenas (above right and below)

HIJACKING HYAENA

The spotted hyaena eats the hard and chewy bits of a **carcass**. It uses its very strong jaws to crush the bones. The black-backed jackal is often found with the hyaena, slinking about optimistically, awaiting the chance to pounce on a leftover scrap.

MARABOU MISCHIEF

The bald, bare-necked Marabou Stork is another **scavenger** that is often found near **carcasses**. Its beak is not designed to tear through meat, so it has to wait for the vultures to rip off pieces small enough for it to swallow. The Marabou Stork also hangs around rubbish dumps and, during the dry season, can be found at water holes that are drying out, where it feasts on stranded fish.

Spotted hyaena

SMELLY SEDUCTION

Blowflies and fleshflies are attracted to the **carcass** by the stench of rotting meat. They lay their tiny eggs inside the **carcass**, and when these hatch, the **maggots** have all the food they can eat.

Longhorn beetle

THE DECOMPOSERS

The **decomposers** complete the garbage-collection process. They break down or **decompose** the fine **debris** left behind, and the nutrients that result from this process sink into the soil and act as a **fertilizer**, stimulating plant growth. Flies, **maggots**, millipedes and termites are just some of the **decomposers** that help to break down plant and animal matter. Some **decomposers**, like bacteria and **fungi**, are so small they can only be seen under a microscope.

If there were no **decomposers** in the world, we would be way past head height in rubbish!

Earthworm

Do your bit!

Unlike the animals of the Bushveld, humans produce a lot of garbage that can't be broken down easily – plastic, for example, can take up to 450 years to **decompose**! This does not mean that we can't do anything about the waste we produce. Instead of just throwing everything into the bin, separate the glass, plastic and paper and take them to a recycling depot. Remember, too, that vegetable and fruit scraps make great compost – ask your parents to help you start a compost heap in the garden.

JUST FOR FUN

Garden garbage collectors

You can find garbage collectors in your own garden. Look for a dead log or branch in a good stage of **decomposition**. Pick it up by lifting the end furthest away from you in order to avoid any nasty surprises – such as snakes, scorpions and centipedes. Pull off a few strips of bark and see what animals live under it.

DID YOU KNOW . . .?

Dung beetles are an export item.

Because African dung beetles are so good at burying lots of dung quickly, they are being exported to Australia, where they don't have enough dung beetles. Piles of dung lying around provide a breeding ground for flies – and Australia has a huge fly problem. Dung beetles carry tiny mites on their stomachs, which eat fly eggs in dung heaps, thereby helping to keep down the number of flies.

In the Bushveld, even those things that look dead are crawling with life. We wander up to a rotting log and probe it with small sticks. The log is alive with weird and wonderful creepy-crawlies such as woodlice, spiders, ants and millipedes, scuttling about their business. When we look closer at the ground, we notice tiny tunnels, made from a thin layer of mud, weaving in and out of the **decomposing** vegetation. On foot, we follow these seemingly directionless tunnels around, and abruptly find ourselves face to face with a towering mound of hard-packed reddish sand. Welcome to the termites' castle!

Like most castles, the termites' is ruled by a king and queen. From the outside, it looks as if nothing is happening in the mound; but inside, it is a frenzied hive of termite activity. In order to explore the termites' home, we have to imagine that we're their size – as small as an ant. Ready? In we go!

TERRIFIC TERMITES

BIG BUSINESS

A termite family can consist of millions of members. Each termite has a specific role to play within the **colony**, and together they create one of the most effective organisations on earth.

The queen

The soldiers have huge jaws

THE CASTLE

The termite mound is built by the worker termites, which use a regurgitated mixture of sand and **saliva**. The **saliva** acts as a cement, which makes the mound very difficult to break open. If termites were as big as humans, then some termite mounds would be buildings up to nine kilometres high! Although the mound looks solid from the outside, inside it is a maze of passages and chambers. Termites have developed their own highly efficient air-conditioning system: cool air is circulated through the nest via a central chimney and passage-ways, which are kept damp by the termites. What is even more astonishing is that, although they are capable of building these architectural wonders, termites are blind.

Termite mounds come in many different shapes and sizes, forming an integral part of the Bushveld landscape.

THE QUEEN

The queen lies in the royal chamber. She is so fat with eggs that she can easily reach five centimetres in length. Sadly for this queen, she doesn't attend any glamorous balls: her job is strictly to lay eggs – sometimes up to 30 000 a day! Depending on the chemical messages, called **pheromones**, passed on to her from the worker termites in the mound, she will produce either workers, soldiers or future kings and queens. After heavy summer rains, when the ground is soft, thousands of termites leave the mound through special exits, and take to the skies. These are the future kings and queens of new **colonies**. Once they have landed on the ground, the queens attract their kings. They then shed their wings and, in pairs, look for a suitable nest site.

THE SOLDIERS

These termites have huge jaws, which they use to defend the **colony** and to attack intruders. As soon as a soldier termite detects that something is breaking into the nest, it passes on the message by repeatedly tapping the walls of the mound, summoning the entire big-jawed army of soldiers to defend the **colony**.

THE WORKERS

The workers make up the majority of the termites in the mound. They are kept extremely busy, doing lots of different jobs, including building and repairing the mound, **foraging**, looking for water and feeding the soldiers, queen, king and **nymphs**. The food-gatherers build special tunnels (like the ones near the rotting log), which are like highways, and which protect these soft-bodied creatures from the sun and from **predators** while they look for food and water. Some workers even construct **fungus** gardens in the mound. These are made from termite dung that is rolled up and shaped into shelves. The **fungus** that grows on these shelves is mixed with regurgitated food and fed as a vitamin supplement to the **nymphs**, the king and the queen.

The workers

TASTY TERMITES

When termites fly out of their nest after the rains, some people catch these 'flying ants' and fry them in a little fat to make a crunchy termite snack – they taste just like peanuts!

But humans aren't the only ones who enjoy a little termite treat now and again. Many animals, among them blue-headed tree agamas, certain frogs, lizards and birds, enjoy a termite tantaliser – they are, after all, a very nutritious source of food.

Some animals specialize in licking up termites. A bizarre-looking bunch, these animals aren't often seen, as they are mainly **nocturnal**.

THE AARDWOLF

The aardwolf finds termites by using its sense of smell and listening with its big 'radar' ears. It doesn't dig into a mound, but rather seeks out termites, licking them up from the soil surface – in fact, it licks up the termites so quickly that the movement of its tongue can't be seen with the eye! Although the aardwolf has sharp teeth, it doesn't eat anything bigger than a grasshopper. These sharp teeth are used for defence and to protect their young. Sadly, many aardwolves have been shot because some farmers wrongly believe that they are responsible for killing their livestock.

Aardwolf

THE AARDVARK

The odd-looking aardvark moves with its long nose close to the ground when **foraging**, using its excellent sense of smell. Once the aardvark finds a termite nest, it uses its sharp claws as mini spades and very quickly digs into the mound. When the tunnels of the termite mound have been exposed, the aardvark inserts its extra-long tongue and licks up the termites.

THE PANGOLIN

Like the aardvark, the scaly pangolin has a keen sense of smell and sharp claws for digging open termite nests. The pangolin's tongue is even longer that the aardvark's – at full stretch, it is as long as its head and body combined! When the pangolin isn't **foraging**, it tucks its tongue into a special pouch in the throat. Pangolins close their sensitive nostrils, so the termites can't crawl up their nose and bite them. They also have thick eyelids to protect their eyes against the termites' sharp jaws.

Pangolin

Aardvark

DID YOU KNOW...?

The water monitor uses the termite mound as an incubator
When a water monitor female is ready to lay her eggs, she finds a termite mound, scratches it open and lays her eggs inside. The worker termites quickly seal the hole, so the eggs have a secure place to incubate out of sight of **predators**. Once the young hatch and have had their fill of delicious termites, they dig their way out to explore the big, wide world.

Water monitor

TEST YOUR SKILLS

Starting in the queen's royal chamber, can you find your way out of the mound?

Termite mounds make wonderful viewing platforms for all sorts of animals.

Termite mound excavated by an aardvark

START

Blister beetles

We have just explored a termite colony and marvelled at the army of strong-jawed soldiers that defend their fellow termites and their home. So how do other animals, which don't have armies to defend them, protect themselves? The Bushveld is filled with a variety of con artists – tricksters that have developed a whole range of clever and convincing self-defence strategies. They either fool **predators** into believing that they taste really awful and are not worth eating, or they look and behave so badly that they scare **predators** off. Some puff themselves up so they look bigger and more scary than they really are; while others use colours to warn **predators** that they are poisonous and dangerous to eat. And there are those that just hide and keep dead quiet.

SELF DEFENCE

BAFFLING BEHAVIOUR

PLAYING DEAD

Some animals have figured out that if they act dead, the potential **predator** will lose interest. The clever click beetle is an excellent actor: it lies dead-still on its back with its legs pointing stiffly up at the sky. If this doesn't work, and the hungry bird or lizard wants to take a nibble anyway, the click beetle very suddenly flips over, jumping up to one metre off the ground, and then races off at top speed. The stunned **predator** is left behind, stomach rumbling, watching his beetle-meal disappear at top speed.

Click beetle

LARGER THAN LIFE

When danger looms, some animals erect the fur on their neck, which makes them look bigger than they really are. The civet does this to scare away **predators**, erecting its hair to a height of 10 cm. You've probably also seen your dog or cat do this.

Toads and monitors puff themselves up so that they look big and scary.

The Egyptian cobra expands its neck and raises the upper third of its body off the ground. To look even more fearsome, it sways from side to side.

This flapnecked chameleon can also puff itself up to look more threatening

TAKEN BY SURPRISE

It's difficult to see a grasshopper when it is resting in the grass, as its earth-coloured body **camouflages** it so well. But if a ravenous bird approaches it, the grasshopper will suddenly spread its dull-coloured front pair of wings to reveal a brilliant flash of red on its back pair of wings, before leaping away. The stunned bird will be even more confused when the grasshopper lands and folds its wings, hiding its bright colours and simply 'disappearing' back into the grass.

Lizards don't mind losing their tail if it means they can keep their life. If a lizard is attacked, it detaches its tail from its body. The surprised **predator** is left with only the wriggling tail in its mouth, while the lizard hastily makes its escape. Lizards are able to grow a new tail.

Stick insects are also quick to lose a limb – if they are attacked, they drop a leg. They have a special joint near the body that allows them to detach their limbs. After escaping the **predator** with this crafty trick, they simply grow a new leg.

Egyptian cobra

CHEMICAL WARFARE

DANGER SIGNS

Many animals rely on their bold patterns and bright colours to let **predators** know that they are dangerous to eat or have a poisonous bite or sting. These **aposematic** colours are red, white, orange, yellow and black, and occur in different combinations.

Certain colourful ground beetles are armed with special glands on their **abdomen**, and can squirt a strong jet of formic acid at an attacker. They can spray acid in any direction, and as far as 35 cm (that's a little longer than a school ruler). The acid is so strong it can cause blindness in small **predators** such as birds and cats.

Banded rubber frog

The blister beetle certainly lives up to its name: if you touch it, a chemical called cantharidin will leave you with painful blisters on your fingers. But the blister beetle plays fair: its bright yellow and black coloration is a warning that it is dangerous.

The body colours of this grasshopper are aposematic

RAISING A STINK

Any animal that foolishly ventures too close to a polecat is in for a very smelly surprise. If a polecat is scared, it turns its bottom towards its attacker and squirts out a disgusting fluid. The polecat's black-and-white-striped coloration, like the blister beetle's, warns potential **predators** to stay a healthy sniff away.

WILY WEAPONS – ASTONISHING ARMOUR

PLAYING HARD BALL

Hedgehogs simply roll up into a spiny ball when they are threatened.

Pangolins, which are covered with overlapping scales, also roll into a ball. Their scales, which are made of **keratin** (the same substance that makes up our fingernails and rhinos' horns), are so strong and spiny that they can't be penetrated. If you ever see a lion playing with a ball in the Bushveld, it is probably a rolled-up pangolin!

Lioness trying to break through a pangolin's hard scales

SPIKY SPEARS

Porcupines use their sharp quills as weapons, but they don't shoot them at an attacker, as many people think. Rather, they quickly turn around and run backwards, stabbing the quills into the face of the **predator** – usually an unsuspecting lion. The quills break off easily, leaving the **predator** full of painful spines. But porcupines also first give their attackers a warning, by rattling their quills very loudly.

GOING TO GROUND

The poisonous puffadder is one of the most dangerous snakes. It is also quite lazy, and will not bother to get out of the way if you approach it. It will, however, give a deep, hollow warning hiss – so if you hear this, stand dead still and then very, very slowly back away. The puffadder relies on excellent **camouflage** to ambush its prey, lying quite still and waiting for some unsuspecting animal to walk within striking distance.

Porcupine

Puffadder

CRAFTY CAMOUFLAGE

IS IT THE TREE I SEE?

The wily bush snake lives in shrubs, bushes and trees. Its green skin blends well into the foliage, and makes it easy for the snake to ambush its **prey**. When threatened, it may inflate its neck, thereby exposing a bright blue colour between the scales. It feeds mainly on lizards, geckos and frogs. It is not dangerous to humans.

Can you spot the Scops Owl and stick insect above and tree agama below?

The **nocturnal** Scops Owl has a feather pattern that resembles the bark of a tree, which is just as well, as it hides away in trees during the day. If alarmed, the owl will straighten up and become long and stiff, looking just like a broken tree stump.

Stick insects are so named for a good reason: it is very difficult to tell the difference between a stick and a stick insect! These insects resemble sticks and twigs because they have thorn-like outgrowths and stick-coloured bodies. Like the bush snake, they make the most of their **camouflage** by swaying gently with the breeze, or sticking out at strange angles, just like the twigs around them.

The **nocturnal** bark spider is very hard-working: it takes down its web every morning, and rebuilds it again every night. During the day it hides against the bark of a tree, where it is so well **camouflaged** that it's almost impossible to detect.

Bark spider

DID YOU KNOW . . .?

Tortoises, such as the leopard tortoise, have a quick and easy defence when they are threatened by a bird or other **predator**: they simply pull in their head and limbs and hide in their shell.

Leopard tortoise

PUZZLING PATTERNS

Have you noticed that when a herd of zebra stand together, it is difficult to see where one animal begins and the next one ends? This is because the zebras' stripes break up the outlines of the animals, which confuses **predators**. Each zebra has its own stripe pattern, just as we each have our very own fingerprints.

The patches on a giraffe's coat do a similar job to the zebras' stripes, helping to interrupt its outline. The patches blend in with dappled light and shade among trees, making the giraffe hard to see.

The rosettes on a leopard's coat also help in breaking up the animal's outline. The leopard's markings are great **camouflage**: when a leopard is resting in a tree, it is almost impossible to detect.

Baby lions have spotted coats, which help to **camouflage** them when they are small. As they grow older and stronger, and more able to defend themselves, the spots disappear.

Patterning on the coats of giraffe (top), zebra (above left) and leopard (above right) provides useful camouflage

MISTAKEN IDENTITY

In order to avoid becoming a lunchtime snack, some animals have, over time, managed to copy the behaviour, shape or colour of poisonous or dangerous animals. These harmless, and usually tasty **mimics**, are left alone by **predators** because they look similar to the more dangerous and poisonous **species**.

Caterpillars are a favourite food of birds – but a hungry bird is less likely to take on a snake than a caterpillar. So processionary caterpillars pretend to be a snake by walking along nose-to-tail, one behind the other. If any one caterpillar steps out of line, the illusion will be shattered and the caterpillars risk being gobbled up by birds.

The female mocker swallowtail butterfly (left) mimics the monarch butterfly (below)

Nose-to-tail, processionary caterpillars look like one giant snake

Monarch butterflies are poisonous. The caterpillars of the butterflies feed on poisonous milkweed plants and can store the poisons in their bodies. Birds can recognize these dangerous butterflies, and leave them well alone. The harmless mocker swallowtail female **mimics** the poisonous monarch butterfly, and so also avoids becoming a bird's breakfast.

When cheetah cubs are small and vulnerable, the markings on their coats resemble those of the honey badger. Honey badgers are well known as ferocious fighters – they will even take on a lion and win.

JUST FOR FUN

Play a game of animal charades. You'll have to observe animals closely to see how they behave. Let's see what a good **mimic** you are – how well can you imitate an elephant feeding with its trunk or a click beetle lying on its back.

Hide and seek

Find out for yourself how **camouflage** makes things hard to find.

WHAT YOU'LL NEED
20 stones of different sizes
blue, red, green, yellow, brown and black paints
a friend who wants some fun

WHAT TO DO
1. Paint each of the 20 stones in different colours and patterns. Make some similar to the **camouflaged** animals we've seen in this chapter – paint some with bright colours, some with spots and some with stripes.
2. Hide them in your garden. (Remember where you've hidden them!)
3. See how long it takes your friend to find them, and note which colours and patterns were found first, and which last.

It is well into the afternoon now, and it has become very hot and sticky. Grey-black thunder-clouds that look like giant mushrooms are forming on the horizon. A little black and white bird whizzes past us and lands on a nearby rock. It is a Fiscal Flycatcher, another **mimic**, which looks very much like that little bully-bird, the Fiscal Shrike. Many birds have been attacked by Fiscal Shrikes, which are very **territorial**, and have learnt to stay clear of these cheeky, hook-beaked birds. Because the harmless, timid Fiscal Flycatcher looks so like the fierce Fiscal Shrike, **predators** and other birds also tend to avoid the flycatcher.

Exploring the world of birds offers a whole Bushveld adventure on its own. Although it takes some time and practice, identifying birds is great fun.

Fiscal Flycatcher

FEATHERED FRIENDS

THE BUSHVELD BIRD IDENTIKIT

When you spot a bird, use the clue kit below to help you identify the bird:
- How big is the bird?
- What shape and colour is its beak?
- What shape and colour are its legs and feet?
- Does it have any bold markings or colours?
- Where did you see it – in a tree, on the ground, or close to water?
- What was the bird doing?

Fiscal Shrike

HOW BIG IS THE BIRD?

The size of a bird is important for identification – is it bigger or smaller than a dove? If it's smaller than a dove, it might, for instance, be a sparrow. If it's about the same size as a dove, it might be a starling; if it's bigger than a dove, it might be a guineafowl; and if it's much bigger than a dove, it might be an eagle.

Scarlet-chested Sunbird

Masked Weaver

Bateleur

WHAT SHAPE IS ITS BEAK?

The shape and size of a bird's beak will tell you not only what **species** the bird might be, but also what it eats. A **raptor**, such as a Martial Eagle or a Bateleur, has a large, hooked bill for tearing meat. A sunbird, on the other hand, has a curved bill to probe into flowers and collect nectar. And a Masked Weaver has a strong, cone-shaped beak, which it uses to crack open seeds.

Hadeda Ibis

Carmine Bee-eater

THE TOUCH-BUTTON BEAK

The Hadeda Ibis has a long, curved beak with extremely sensitive touch receptors at the tip. It feeds by walking along slowly, probing the grass or mud with its beak. It uses its 'touch button' to pick up any movement of live **prey** such as worms in the soil.

Barbet

THE TWEEZER BEAK

Bee-eaters are among the most beautiful birds in the Bushveld. They are also the bravest, as they enjoy eating bees! The Carmine Bee-eater catches the bee with its long, beak, then rubs the bee against a branch until all the venom in the bee's sting has come out. Then it simply gulps down the bee whole.

THE CHISELLING BEAK

Barbets and woodpeckers have a short, strong beak that they use as chisels for extracting **prey** from wood, as well as for excavating nests. The woodpecker also has a sticky tongue, which is twice as long as its beak. It uses its tongue to probe into holes in tree trunks and branches to extract any juicy **prey** (woodborer **larvae** are a favourite).

WHAT SHAPE AND COLOUR ARE ITS FEET AND LEGS?

Like beaks, feet come in different shapes, depending on what they are used for. **Raptors**, for instance, have large, claw-like talons to grasp and kill their **prey**. Waterbirds such as the African Jacana often have long toes, which help to spread their weight on aquatic plants. This enables them to walk on floating leaves without sinking.

TRICKY TOES

The Black Egret has bright yellow toes, which it uses when it goes fishing. It stands in the water and wriggles its colourful toes, and this attracts nosy fish. The egret then pounces on the unsuspecting fish and enjoys a fresh dinner.

GYMNASTIC JOINTS

The Gymnogene eats young birds from the nests of weavers and sparrows. It uses its double-jointed legs to reach into the nests to grasp its **prey**.

FEATHERED LEGS

True eagles, such as the Black Eagle, are the only **raptors** that have feathers on their legs.

Black Egret

African Jacana

Gymnogen

*African
Fish Eagle*

DOES IT HAVE ANY BOLD MARKINGS OR COLOURS?

A bird's markings and colours can be a good clue as to what **species** it is. The Lilac-breasted Roller, for example, has a pink and blue chest; the Masked Weaver has a black head and the Martial Eagle has a white tummy. Look closely: does the bird have colour on its wings, tail, head or chest? Does it have any bold markings, such as black bands across its tail?

Martial Eagle

WHERE DID YOU SEE IT?

Birds choose specific areas to live in, and where they live depends on the available food, shelter and nesting sites. This is known as their **habitat**.

LOFT LIVING

Within these **habitats**, different **species** of birds feed at different levels of the environment, much the same as the **herbivores'** multi-storey restaurant. Eagles will almost certainly be found at the top of a tree, waiting for a good thermal (warm air current) on which they can fly off, while guineafowl **forage** at ground level, and woodpeckers can be found scurrying around the trunks of trees.

Guineafowl feather

WHAT WAS THE BIRD DOING?

What a bird is doing can also help you to identify what **species** it is. For example, was it swimming, hovering, or flying from tree to tree? If it's in a tree, look a little closer: is it perched on an outer branch of the tree, **hawking** insects as they fly past (in which case it might be a bee-eater), or is it scurrying around the trunk (in which case it might be a woodpecker)?

Lilac-breasted Roller

NEST NEWS

Different birds build different kinds of nests in different places, and this can also help you identify what kind of bird it is that you are looking at. Nests can be very simple, like the reed nest of the African Jacana; or really complicated, like that of a Hamerkop, which can reach a height of over two metres!

African Jacana nest

FUSSY FEMALES

The Masked Weaver has to work very hard to attract a mate. He impresses the female by building her a nest in which she can start their family. Unfortunately, it seems that female Masked Weavers aren't all that easy to please! On many occasions the female will carefully inspect the nest – and then simply reject it! The poor male then has to pull the nest apart and start all over again.

And it isn't an easy business: this little bird has to fly over 200 kilometres to collect around 800 pieces of new nest material. Really fussy Masked Weaver females may reject a male's nest up to seven times before she finally decides it's good enough for her to lay her precious eggs in.

Masked Weaver

THE HOLE TRUTH

The next time you see a Yellow-billed Hornbill with an insect in its mouth, flying towards a tree, don't be too surprised if it looks as though it is feeding the tree! But look a little closer: do you see it pushing that insect into a slit in the trunk? And who's behind that slit? It is the male hornbill's family, of course.

When the female hornbill is ready to lay her eggs, she finds a suitably sized hollow in a tree and then seals herself into it using mud, bark, leaves and her own drop-

Yellow-billed Hornbill

pings. Then she lays her eggs. While she is in the hollow, sitting on her eggs, she loses most of her feathers, which are thought to be used as a lining for the nest. Once the young have hatched, the male is responsible for feeding the hungry family. And when the chicks are half grown, the mother leaves the nest and they reseal it, and continue to be fed by their parents until they are nearly fully grown.

Hamerkop nest

Red-chested Cuckoo

CARELESS CUCKOOS

Cuckoos certainly aren't going to win any prizes for parenting – they don't take any part in raising their chicks at all. The Red-chested Cuckoo, for example, lays its eggs in the nests of other birds, such as the Cape Robin, and then takes no further part in the rearing of the chicks. In many cases, the eggs that the cuckoos lay are perfect copies of the **host's** eggs. Guess what happens next? The cuckoo chick hatches and, to add insult to injury, often kicks the **host's** chicks out of the nest! The cuckoo chick often grows much bigger than its 'parent', who has to work extremely hard to keep its huge 'baby' fed.

THE PERFECT PACKAGE

The colouring of the egg usually serves a purpose – as a rule, eggs that are laid in open nests on the ground, such as plovers' eggs, are well **camouflaged**, while eggs that are laid in an enclosed nest, such as the bee-eaters' tunnel in an embankment, are often plain and white. It is thought that these eggs are white so that they are visible in the dark nest and stand less chance of being damaged.

Plover eggs

Attract birds to your garden

All birds enjoy a place where they can rest, nest, feed and drink. Create a menu that birds won't be able to resist. Remember that each bird has different requirements. Once you've made a bird table that is secure, lay out leftover bacon rind, fat or bonemeal for the insect eaters. The fruit eaters will relish any fruit and the seed eaters will appreciate birdseed as well as porridge. In no time, word will be out that your bird table has the tastiest menu!

DID YOU KNOW ...?

Ostrich eggs have their own built-in air-conditioning.
Ostriches lay light-coloured eggs in their open nests, which can easily be spotted by **predators**. So why are their eggs not **camouflaged**? The answer has to do with keeping cool. In a hot, dry environment, the creamy colour and glossy surface of the eggs prevent them from overheating – the light colour of the eggs is a trade-off between the risk of being snatched away by a **predator**, or overheating when the eggs are left unattended. Finding and eating an ostrich egg is a real treat – one egg is equal to 24 hen's eggs!

The clouds are now looming overhead. Deafening thunder rumbles across the landscape and all around us the animals become very still. It is as if the Bushveld is holding its breath, waiting for the first raindrops to fall. But listen: one bird has continued calling. From its call - a monotonous 'pink, pink, pink' - we can tell that it's a Yellow-fronted Tinker Barbet. It is a very elusive little bird and is not often seen, but by learning its call we can identify it straight away. Why do birds sing so much? You might think it's just because they're happy, but birds actually use their calls for many purposes: to find mates, to alert other birds of danger, to communicate with their chicks, and to warn off invaders of their **territory**. Sound is not the only way animals pass on messages. They communicate by sight and smell too. Some animals leave smelly messages on plants. The Bushveld is full of nature's signposts.

Yellow-fronted Tinker Barbet

NATURE'S SIGNPOSTS

HEAR, HERE
The Bushveld can provide a symphony of sound. Animals are in constant contact with each other – to keep in touch and to defend their **territory**.

A male lion has such a loud roar, it can be heard up to eight kilometres away! Males claim and defend their **territories** by emitting very loud roars, which serve to keep out of that particular range all but the bravest competitors.

The Cardinal Woodpecker 'knocks' by tapping very fast with its bill on a dead branch. This sound, which carries a lot further than its call, tells other woodpeckers that the **territory** is occupied.

One of the most common sounds in the Bushveld is that of the male cicada beetle, which drums in the heat of the day. It makes this sound by vibrating a tight membrane on its **abdomen**.

SENDING SCENTS

There are different ways of marking a **territory** with a smelly message.

Some buck leave a message to tell other buck that the **territory** is occupied by rubbing a special gland on their face, called a pre-orbital gland, against trees and shrubs. The substance from the gland can remain on the plant for a long time. They also have a gland in their feet called a pedal gland. This gland leaves a scent trail that marks out the buck's **territory**.

Hyaenas secrete a paste from their anal gland onto grass stalks. This paste leaves a message for other hyaenas – telling them, for example, whether it was a male or a female hyaena, if it was a hyaena from the same **clan** or a complete stranger, and how long ago the animal was there. This message can last for over a month.

Cardinal Woodpecker

Male rhinos mark their **territory** by squirting urine on the ground. They also walk through their dung, so that as they move around their **territory**, they leave the smell of their dung behind. This tells other rhinos to stay out of their particular home.

Bushbabies urinate on their hands and in this way leave smelly handprints on all the trees within their **territory**.

SEEING IS BELIEVING

'Animal toilets' are places where certain animals go to leave their dung. They often make the toilet out in an open area for all to see. This is a sign showing others that the area is occupied. A **herbivore** toilet is called a 'midden', while the **carnivores'** and **omnivores'** is called a 'latrine'.

A rhino midden

Rhinos mark their territory in different ways; here dispersing dung and urine to say 'keep out'!

The hippo scatters its dung far and wide by vigorously flicking its short, flat tail sideways. The dung can accumulate into heaps half a metre deep!

Cats use trees as scratching posts to keep their claws in shape. At the same time, they mark a tree for all to see.

Cheetah

The male Fiscal Shrike, also known as a 'Jackie Hanger', spikes dead insects onto the thorns of acacia trees. He does this to show the female that he is a good hunter and will make a suitable mate.

TELLING TAILS

Some of nature's signposts warn that there is danger about. Certain animals use their tails to do this.

As soon as a warthog senses trouble, it sticks its tail straight up in the air like an aerial. That is why the Shangaans call them 'radio-controlled pigs'. When they are running for safety, the warthogs can keep each other in sight by following each others' tails.

Warthog

It is thought that the black tip on the tail of the mother lion is also a following signal for her cubs, as lions can only see in black and white. The backs of the ears are also black, and this following signal is used when adult lions are hunting together.

Lioness and cub

The waterbuck has a white oval ring around its tail – it looks as if it has just sat on a freshly painted toilet seat! This ring serves as a following signal for the herd to stick together when danger approaches.

Kudu female

When threatened, certain antelope, such as kudu, lift their tails to show the white fluffy underside. When the kudu is running through thick bush, this flash of white can easily be seen as a marker for the herd to follow.

Waterbuck male

SCRATCH PATCH
Elephants enjoy wallowing in mud. After the hot sun dries the mud on their backs, their skin tends to get a bit itchy and they go off to find a tree, where they will have a good hearty scratch. Over time, these scratching posts can easily be recognized as elephant signposts by the smooth and worn bark of the tree and the bits of old dried mud sticking to it.

Elephant feeding

Trees can also be recognizable signposts, as elephants scrape off and eat the bark from trees – it makes a delicious, if chewy, snack.

A scratching post

DID YOU KNOW ...?
You can sometimes tell if an animal is male or female by looking at its droppings.
It is often possible to identify whether an animal is male or female by looking at its wet urine patch in relation to its dung. A male's urine is deposited forward of the dung heap, whereas the female's urine lies close to the dung.

The storm has finally broken. As flashes of lightning whip across the sky, we quickly make our way back towards our camp. When the first fat raindrops begin falling, we tilt back our heads and open our mouths to catch them. Dripping, we hasten along and accidentally disturb a herd of kudu in our path – we look on as they run off with their white tails signalling danger.

Some animals carry private 'watchmen' on their backs to warn them of approaching danger. One of these 'watchmen' is a little bird called an oxpecker. In return for warning its 'ride' that there is trouble about, the bird gets its food, in the form of ticks and lice, from the hide of the animal.

But this is not the only type of friendship in the Bushveld. The most unlikely animals may end up sharing homes together, and in some cases, they even share tasty treats!

FASCINATING FRIENDSHIPS

TICK TIME

The oxpecker feeds on tasty ticks. Once it has found a tick-infested friend such as a buffalo, the oxpecker combs the buffalo's fur with its scissor-like beak, pulling off a bounty of nutritious ticks. In return for its dinner (and for the animal's soft hair, which it uses to line its nest), the oxpecker warns the buffalo of any potential danger by giving its warning call, which is a loud churring, hissing sound.

TICK FOR TAT

Impalas use the thin second and third incisor teeth as a 'comb' to remove ticks from their fur. But because an impala can't reach its own neck and head with its teeth, it will call on the help of another impala to clean these areas. The two impala will stand face to face, giving each other a thorough de-ticking.

TICK TAKE-OUTS

Terrapins often swim up to animals that quench their thirst at a waterhole. These crafty terrapins pluck off ticks and any old skin from the forelegs of thirsty animals. In this way, terrapins have dinner delivered to their doorstep, while the visitor gets rid of its annoying pests and **parasites**.

Terrapin plucking ticks from a kudu

Terrapin

SWEET TREATS

Ants, honeyguides and honey badgers specialize in collecting delicious treats from the Bushveld, and all have special friends that help them do this.

The larval stage (or caterpillar) of the little blue butterfly has a fascinating friendship with certain ant species. The caterpillar excretes a substance called honeydew, which is rich in sugars and nutrients, on which the ants feed. In return for this sweet treat, the ants will take the caterpillar into their nest, protecting it from **predators** such as birds.

The honeyguide is very well named – this little bird has led animals, including humans, to beehives for centuries. It has a special friendship with the honey badger which, as its name suggests, also loves honey. The honeyguide will fly ahead of the honey badger, guiding it to a beehive, stopping on bushes and waiting every so often, while the honey badger catches up. Once there, the honey badger will use its sharp claws to break open the hive. Its thick, hairy coat protects it from the stings of the bad-tempered bees. The honey badger, a very sloppy eater, will enjoy its Bushveld buffet of sticky honey, and will leave crunchy bee larvae and mouth-watering beeswax over for the honeyguide to gobble up.

Honey badgers feeding from a bees' nest

Honey badger and honeyguide

The shape of the sunbird's beak is adapted to that of the tubular flower

FLOWER POWER

When feeding from aloe plants, certain sunbirds act as **pollinators**. When the sunbird dips its curved beak into the tubular flower and drinks the nectar, **pollen** from the flowers rubs off on its beak. The sunbird then moves on to another flower, and in this way carries **pollen** to other plants.

Baobabs and bats have a similar relationship. Baobab flowers open at night, and certain fruitbats visit the blooms. During these night flights, the bats carry pollen from flower to flower.

BIZARRE BEDMATES

Porcupines and warthogs share a deep burrow for safety. You might think that the warthog would not appreciate this prickly arrangement, but it actually works well – for both animals. The warthog is **diurnal** and leaves the porcupine to sleep in the burrow during the day. The porcupine, on the other hand, is **nocturnal**, so it leaves the warthog sleeping peacefully when it goes out at night.

Have you ever watched a warthog entering its burrow? It goes in bottom first. The fable goes like this: many years ago, the warthog went in head first, only to crash into the porcupine, who hadn't yet left the burrow. The poor warthog ended up with painful porcupine quills stuck into its face – which explains all the ugly warts and bumps it has on its face to this day! And this is why the warthog always reverses into its burrow: in case the porcupine is still at home!

Warthog burrow

NEIGHBOURHOOD WATCH

Blue wildebeest and Burchell's zebra often graze together. This is because Burchell's zebra have excellent eyesight and wildebeest have very sharp hearing – and a **predator** would have to be very wily if he wanted to sneak up on such a good team!

Impala live in large herds for similar reasons: the more eyes and ears there are, the less likely it is that a **predator** can spring a surprise attack.

Grey Lourie

Zebra and blue wildebeest

Many birds act as 'watchmen', warning all animals in the area when danger is approaching. The Grey Lourie, which is also known as the 'Go-away Bird', quickly alerts neighbouring animals with its piercing 'Go away!' call.

Monkeys and baboons often **forage** near the tops of trees. From this high vantage point, they can keep an eye on everything that's happening down below, and give the neighbourhood early warning.

Yellow-billed Hornbill

Chacma baboon

DID YOU KNOW...?

Dwarf mongooses and Yellow-billed Hornbills are friends.

Dwarf mongooses and Yellow-billed Hornbills often **forage** together for food. As the mongoose scratches through the soil for insects, some escape, which the hornbill snaps up. They also watch out for one another: the hornbill keeps an eye on the sky while the mongoose is foraging, and warns the mongoose if a hungry **raptor** flies overhead; while the mongoose is good at sniffing out ground-based **predators**, such as large grey mongooses, and warns the hornbill if one is around.

Sometimes a hungry hornbill might even call loudly down the burrow of a dozing mongoose, to wake up its friend and make sure that dinner will be served!

Dwarf mongooses

*J*ust as suddenly as the storm arrived, it has gone, leaving a thin layer of moisture on the ground to trap the dust. The fresh, rich scent of wet soil and damp air fills our noses. The sky looks very dramatic as the last rays of the setting sun catch the edge of the dispersing purple thunderclouds. The familiar call of Natal Francolins drifts through the bush as they find a suitable place to roost for the night. In fact, all the animals seem very busy finding a quiet, safe place at the end of the day.

As we carry on towards our camp, a little tired now, we play a game of 'I spy with my little eye' – and we soon realize that many different kinds of eyes are peering at us out of the dense bush.

I SPY WITH MY LITTLE EYE

SPY EYES

Different animals have their eyes positioned at different places on their heads. Let's see why.

EYES ON TOP OF THEIR HEADS

Hippos and crocodiles have their eyes, ears and noses on the top of their heads. This allows them to hide below the water's surface, yet at the same time be able to see, hear and smell things above the water.

SIDEWAYS-LOOKING EYES

Animals with eyes on either side of their head, such as Burchell's zebra, can see almost everything that is happening around them, making it difficult for a **predator** such as a lion to catch them unawares.

FORWARD-LOOKING EYES

Many animals that have forward-looking eyes are **predators**, such as hyaenas and lions. The position of their eyes allows them accurately to work out the distance to their **prey**. The downside is, of course, that these animals cannot see what is happening behind them.

Burchell's zebra with sideways-looking eyes

LOOK AGAIN!

Some animals use eye patterns for scaring and deceiving **predators**.

Some butterflies, such as little blues, have two heads – or so it seems. In fact, they have developed a 'false head' at the tips of their hindwings. A **foraging** bird might mistakenly grab the false head, and the butterfly can then flutter off, leaving only a little of its wing in the puzzled bird's mouth.

Little blue butterfly

The emperor moth has a pair of frightening-looking 'eyespots' tucked away behind its wings. When danger approaches, the moth quickly jumps forward and reveals these large and intimidating 'eyes'. This confuses the hungry bird or lizard long enough for the moth to make its hasty escape.

Spotted hyaena

Emperor moth

JUST FOR FUN

Take a close look at the eyes of the animals around you – your dog's, your cat's, birds in the garden. Using the above information as clues, work out if they are **nocturnal** or **diurnal**, and whether they are **herbivores** or **predators**.

Eye test

Humans have binocular vision, which means we need both of our eyes to properly judge depth and distance. Test it for yourself.

WHAT YOU'LL NEED
1 cup
1 coin
a helpful friend

WHAT TO DO
Put the cup on a table and stand about three metres (three big steps) away from it. Cover one of your eyes with your hand. Ask a friend to hold out a coin and slowly move it around above the cup. When you think that the coin is directly above the cup and will fall into it if it's dropped, ask your friend to drop it.

Did the coin fall into the cup? Good chance it didn't. This is because you are using only one eye, so your binocular vision isn't working.

Now try it again with both of your eyes and see if your aim improves.

Pearl-spotted Owl – front (left) and back (right)

The Pearl-spotted Owl has two dark, round spots at the back of its head, which, from a distance, look like eyes. This has the useful effect of making the owl look as if it has eyes in the back of its head! A would-be attacker, for example a genet, feels that it is being watched no matter from which direction it approaches the owl.

NIGHT EYES
Nocturnal animals have eyes that are specially adapted so that they can see well in the dark.

Some **nocturnal** animals, such as genets, have eyes that shine when a spotlight is pointed at them. This is due to a mirror-like layer at the back of each eye, which reflects the light back into the eyes. The retina (which is the light-sensitive membrane in the eye that allows us to see) then has a second chance to pick up any light missed the first time round.

Genet

Some **nocturnal** cats, such as leopards, civets and lions, have distinct pale markings under their eyes. It's thought that these markings help reflect all the available light into the animals' eyes at night, giving them an advantage over their **prey**.

Leopard

Many **nocturnal** animals, such as owls and bushbabies, have large eyes, which enable them to capture any starlight or moonlight available. This allows them to locate their **prey** more efficiently.

Bushbabies' eyes are so big, in fact, that their eyes are almost incapable of movement within the socket! To make up for this, they can swivel their heads almost entirely round.

Mozambique spitting cobra

SEE-THROUGH SUNGLASSES

Snakes and geckos do not have movable eyelids. Instead, the eyelids have joined together to form a see-through 'spectacle' over the eye. This is what gives the snake its frozen, glassy gaze. In the case of the gecko, if the 'spectacle' happens to get dirty, a quick swipe with the tongue clears the picture – much like a windscreen wiper!

Compound eyes of a dragon-fly

Compound eyes of a praying mantid

HOW MANY EYES HAVE I?

One would think that most animals have only two eyes, but that is not always the case. There are many examples where an animal has more eyes than meets the eye!

Insects have two types of eyes: a large pair of compound eyes and then up to three simple eyes too. The simple eyes are equipped with lenses but are used for detecting changes in the light rather than seeing objects.

The compound eyes are made up of hundreds to thousands of different parts, each having a lens and a nerve connection to the brain. They are specially designed to pick up quick movement and judge distance, which explains why a fly is so hard to swat!

DID YOU KNOW ...?

There's a beetle with four eyes.

The whirligig beetle, which looks like a little speed-boat, lives in rivers. Each of its eyes is divided into two halves, so that it can see both above and below the water at the same time. This means that it can look for food and also keep an eye out for danger.

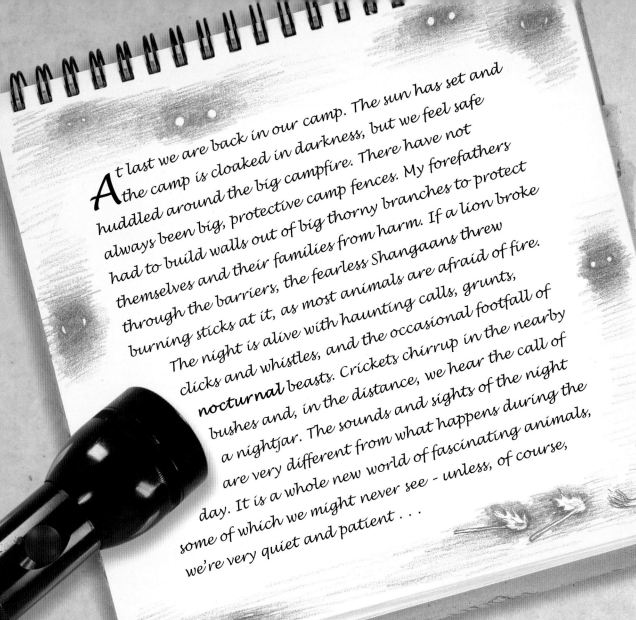

At last we are back in our camp. The sun has set and the camp is cloaked in darkness, but we feel safe huddled around the big campfire. There have not always been big, protective camp fences. My forefathers had to build walls out of big thorny branches to protect themselves and their families from harm. If a lion broke through the barriers, the fearless Shangaans threw burning sticks at it, as most animals are afraid of fire. The night is alive with haunting calls, grunts, clicks and whistles, and the occasional footfall of **nocturnal** beasts. Crickets chirrup in the nearby bushes and, in the distance, we hear the call of a nightjar. The sounds and sights of the night are very different from what happens during the day. It is a whole new world of fascinating animals, some of which we might never see - unless, of course, we're very quiet and patient . . .

THE NIGHT SHIFT

WHOSE EYES ARE THOSE?

The eyes of night creatures seen in the torchlight might look really strange, but there are clues you can use to work out which animal is behind the eyes.

LARGE RED EYES, LOOKING FORWARD, AND APPEARING TO JUMP

These are the eyes of bushbabies, which reflect a reddish colour as they jump among the branches of the trees.

African wildcat

'HEADLIGHT' EYES THAT SHINE GREEN AND WHITE, MOVING CLOSE TO THE GROUND

These are the eyes of little **predators**, such as civets, genets and African wildcats.

The civet's eyes shine a beautiful emerald green in the torchlight as they search the ground for small animals, fruit and insects. Their claim to fame is their scent, which is used to mark their **territory**. This scent was used many years ago as a base in the perfume industry but has now been replaced with a man-made equivalent.

The African wildcat looks similar to a domestic cat. Unfortunately, there are very few genetically pure wildcats left, as they have cross-bred with domestic cats. The large-spotted genet has big ears, which enable it to pick up on any little rustle on the ground. It also has a long tail that it uses for balancing as it climbs trees looking for birds to eat.

Genet

LARGE EYES, LOOKING FORWARD, AND SHINING A REDDISH COLOUR

These eyes belong to the larger **predators**, such as leopards, lions and hyaenas.

EYES THAT TURN AWAY

Elephants turn their heads away when a torch is shone at them, as they don't like having a bright light shone into their eyes.

GREENISH EYES, WIDELY SPACED

These are an antelope's eyes – you can tell they belong to a **herbivore** because of their position, on either side of the head. They shine a greenish colour in the torchlight.

TINY EYES ON THE GROUND

These are the eyes of the wolf spider, which lies quietly on the ground, waiting to run down its **prey**.

Genet

Leopard in a tree with its dinner

MAGIC LIGHTS

These are fireflies: bright flashing lights, darting here and there in the dark sky – and one of the most beautiful sights at night in the Bushveld. Fireflies use light to communicate. A special organ in the firefly's **abdomen** makes the light, which is flashed to attract a mate. Each **species** of firefly has a different signal. Some female fireflies have devised a terrible trick: they **mimic** the signal of a female of another **species**, and when a male lands to mate with them, he is promptly gobbled up! All male fireflies have wings. The females of some **species** don't have wings; these females are called glowworms.

Firefly

THE NIGHT-TIME SYMPHONY

If you fine-tune your hearing at night, you will soon be able to work out who's making what sound.

HUSH LITTLE BABY

If you hear the sound of a baby crying in the Bushveld, don't be too surprised. It is a bushbaby, and it uses its cry to defend its **territory** and communicate with other bushbabies. Bushbabies are **arboreal**, and can jump huge distances between trees – sometimes as much as ten times their own height! Their favourite food is the gum of the sweet thorn tree, and they also eat insects.

Bushbabies clean themselves and other bushbabies with a special tooth that acts as a comb. They sleep during the day in family groups of up to seven individuals, all curled up together in the hollow of a tree.

GOSPEL SINGER

The Fiery-necked Nightjar is a bird that has the most beautiful night call. It sounds like, 'Good Lord, deliver us.' Flying through the air, nightjars use their mouth like a huge net to catch insects. The whiskers on the sides of their beak help them feel for insects as they fly.

Lesser bushbaby

Fiery-necked Nightjar

TU-WHIT, TU-WHOO

Each owl **species** has its own distinctive call, which they make at night. Under the cover of darkness, they hunt for their **prey**, which can include mice, small mammals and frogs. They have certain **adaptations** that enable them to do this. Many owls have the feathers on their face arranged in such a way that they capture sound and channel it into the owl's ears. They also have much larger ear openings than other birds. These ear openings are not at the same level on either side of the head, and owls can pick up how far away their **prey** is by receiving sound at slightly different times.

Pearl-spotted Owls

CLICKETY-CLACK

Insect-eating bats find their **prey** using echolocation. As the bats fly, they produce a metallic sound in their throat, which is projected forward. When this sound hits a solid object, it bounces back from the object and into the ears of the bat. The bat's brain then deciphers the reflected sound and works out what the object is. This is a very effective way of catching **prey** at night – one bat can catch up to 600 mosquitoes in a single hour!

CHIRPY CHIRRUPS

Male crickets have specially developed areas on the wings, which they rub together – the chirruping sound that crickets make is actually caused by the vibrations of this rubbing.

Insect-eating bat

NOISE AT NIGHT

The black-backed jackal uses its 'Nyaaaaa ya ya ya!' call to mark its **territory**, to fend off intruders and to find a mate. Black-backed jackals have a variety of other calls too, but they will always keep silent when following hunting lions, until the lions have made a successful kill. Then they will call their friends and family to join the feast.

JUST FOR FUN

Humans are **diurnal**, and don't have any **adaptations** to allow them to see well at night. If the night is really dark, we have to rely more on our ears than our eyes. Cup your hands behind your ears and listen to how your hearing improves. Then cup your hands in front of your ears to hear what is happening behind you.

Black-backed jackal

Gecko

CREEPY-CRAWLY CAMP CREATURES

Many little creatures come into our camp at night. Some are harmless, but there are others that may not be very welcome!

MOONSTRUCK

Ever wondered why **nocturnal** insects fly towards lights at night? Many insects use the light of the moon to tell them where they are going, so when they see a bright light, they think it is the moon and fly towards it. Entomologists, who are people who study insects, often use lights to attract and trap **nocturnal** specimens.

GRACEFUL GECKOS

Geckos often feed at night on those insects that are attracted to camp lights. Geckos have very small hairs on their feet that enable them to stick to anything, which explains how they can climb up a smooth wall so easily.

SLENDER SERPENTS

Night adders enjoy eating toads and frogs. They use poison to kill their **prey**. These snakes can reach one metre in length.

SCARY SCORPIONS

Scorpions, such as the burrowing scorpion, are mostly active on windy nights. They use their pincers to catch insects and then use their sting to poison them.

You can tell if a scorpion is venomous by looking at the size of its tail in relation to its pincers. If the scorpion's tail is thin and the pincers are large, then it is not too dangerous. If, however, its tail is fat and its pincers are small, stay away!

Always remember to check your shoes in the morning before you put them on, as scorpions enjoy crawling into or under something to pass away the day.

A thin-tailed scorpion

Night adder

DID YOU KNOW . . .?

Baby scorpions ride on their mother's back.
Certain young scorpions catch a piggy-back ride on the backs of their mothers. At this stage they are only a few millimetres long, and there can be as many as 90 young ones catching a ride at the same time! They stay safely on their mom's back until their first **moult**.

TEST YOUR SKILLS

Imagine you are out in the Bushveld with only the moon shining down on you. You shine your torch into the ink-black darkness, and find different coloured pairs of eyes, and lights, sparkling back at you. How many of these **nocturnal** animals can you spot: fireflies, lions, bushbabies, impalas, wolf spiders, African wildcats?

* Answers on p 63.

Snug in our sleeping bags, we lie listening to the lions roaring and the whoop of the spotted hyaena. Above us, a billion brilliant stars seem so close to us that we could almost reach out and touch them. As you close your eyes and get ready to fall asleep, I complete the day with a story. The Shangaans lived off the land, in perfect balance with nature, until Western men arrived. From then on, the wilderness was never the same. The new-comers did many things that puzzled the Shangaans. They killed wild animals, not to eat them, but to sell their skins and ivory. Slowly, the ancient Shangaan knowledge of the wild started losing its value. Preserving natural areas is imperative to our future, but we also need to consider the people living close to these areas. It is an intricate balance, one that we need to respect and look after. All the animals and plants that we have admired today depend on one another in the great circle of life.

JABU'S WISH

I hope that today's experiences have shown you that there is another, truly wondrous, world out there. A beautiful sunset to gladden your heart, the friendship you hear in a bird's call, the amazing things you can discover in the Bushveld if you only take the time and trouble to look close enough – take these experiences with you as gifts to treasure. And never forget that it's up to each one of us to make sure that we continue to share our planet with everything and everyone that lives on it. It lies in your hands. Look at what you have discovered today and then make a promise that you will try to do at least one thing when you get home that will change how we use our world – for the better.

YOUR DISCOVERIES

- We can achieve far more when we work together, just as the animals do in **Fascinating Friendships**.
- It doesn't matter how small you are or how small your contribution is, it all adds up and makes a difference. Look at the **Terrific Termites**: even though they're small, they build mounds as big as mountains.
- Tread lightly on the planet. If humans left behind only footprints, rather than destruction, man and the wilderness would be able to exist harmoniously together.
- As long as we care for each other and share with each other, there will be enough to go around for everyone. If the herbivores can do it in their **Multi-storey Restaurant**, so can we!
- We need to re-use, reduce and recycle. Look at how effective the Bushveld **Garbage Collectors** are!

YOUR PROMISE

- I will always switch off the lights when I leave a room, as making electricity creates harmful pollution.
- I will close the tap while I brush my teeth, as water is precious.
- I will give the birds food and water in my garden, as their habitats are being reduced.
- I will take a cloth bag to the shops for small shopping, and if I do use plastic bags that pollute the environment, I'll make sure that I take them to the recycling bin.

BB

Just as BB has buried the precious dung ball containing the future generation, why don't you also gather up all the information in this book and use it wisely for the future conservation of our planet.

CAN YOU FIND . . .?

See how well you have remembered the many animals and plants you have encountered today. In the book, can you find the following?

1. An oxpecker
2. A toothbrush tree
3. The Bushveld gardener
4. Nature's cup
5. A queen termite
6. A scorpion
7. The emperor moth's false eyes
8. A waterbuck
9. A Cape Vulture
10. An antlion track
11. A white rhino marking his territory
12. A Red-chested Cuckoo
13. The Bushveld ladder
14. A spotted hyaena
15. An aardvark
16. A bee-eater
17. A dwarf mongoose
18. A bushbaby
19. An animal with eyes on the side of the head
20. An impala track
21. A lion's ball

ACKNOWLEDGEMENTS

I remain inspired by, and am thankful to Clive Walker for his energy and commitment to environmental education in Southern Africa over the years. It was a privilege to work alongside Hanneke van der Merwe at Lapalala Wilderness Environmental School, who was both a mentor and a friend to me and whose tireless dedication in teaching children in the wild was nothing short of admirable. I would also like to express my sincere appreciation to Shan and Dave Varty for modelling and instilling a vision for the sustainability of our biodiversity in the future and encouraging me to pursue my dreams. To the team that made the book a reality, I extend my gratitude, especially Pippa Parker and Katharina von Gerhardt, who have shared my vision for the book from the outset. I would also like to give thanks to James Marshall and Lex Hes who assisted with photographs, and Bushwillow for the use of their safari clothes and equipment. Last but not least I am indebted to my parents, who planted the wilderness seed in my heart as a child, and to Neil, my husband and soul mate, who has given me so much encouragement and support.

ANSWERS TO QUESTIONS

Keeping Track P. 12
1. Four impala came down to drink at the waterhole.
2. No. Only three impala left the waterhole.
3. The fourth impala was eaten by a crocodile.
4. No, the zebra did not have a drink.
5. Yes, a hungry lion was following the zebra.
6. The rhino had a drink at the waterhole and then walked off.
7. The rhino tracks are not fresh.
8. There is an antlion trail over the rhino tracks. (See magnifying glass.)
9. The rhino walked in a northerly direction.
10. Yes, along the edge of the treeline north of the zebra tracks.
11. Along the north and eastern side of the waterhole.

Multi-storey Restaurant p. 21
1 = B, 3 = C, 2 = A, 4 = D, 5 = E

The Night Shift p. 59
Fireflies: 7, Lion: 1, Impalas: 8, Bushbabies: 3, Wolf spider: 1, Wildcat: 1

PICTURE CREDITS – All pictures Francois Ellis © Nadine Clarke, with the exception of the following:

Shaen Adey/SIL: P. 45 top right
Daryl and Sharna Balfour/SIL: Pp. 3; 34 bottom left; 51 top left
Andrew Bannister/SIL: Pp 19 Bottom right; 20 bottom left; 39 middle and top right; 42 bottom left
Keith Begg/SIL: Pp. 20 bottom right; 29 top middle; 40 top left
Peter Blackwell/SIL: Pp. 34 bottom right; 37 bottom left
Nigel J Dennis/DDP: Pp. 23 bottom; 28 top right; 29 top left; 38 top and bottom left; 52 bottom right
Nigel J Dennis/SIL: Pp. 1 centre; 20 top right; 24 bottom left; 33 middle left and bottom left; 34 top; 36 bottom right; 37 top right middle right and middle left; 39 bottom right; 40 top left and middle right; 44 bottom; 47 middle; 49 bottom left, middle right and top right; 50; 51 middle right; 58 top left

Roger de la Harpe/DDP: Pp. 41 top right; 57 top left
Roger de la Harpe/SIL: Pp. 19 bottom left; 57 bottom right
Richard du Toit: Pp. 23 middle; 38 bottom right; 43 middle right; 55 top left
Albert Froneman: Pp. 24 bottom right; 41 top left; 43 top right; 56 bottom
Charles Griffiths: Pp. 22 top left; 25 middle left and top left; 43 top left; 51 middle left; 56 top right (Mike Picker)
Lex Hes: Pp. 4; 5; 8 top; 9 middle right; 19 top and middle left; 20 middle left; 22 bottom; 23 top; 24 top left, right and middle; 26; 27; 28 middle left and bottom left; 29 top right and bottom right; 30 top left; 31 middle left and bottom right; 32 top right and bottom left; 33 top left and top middle; 35 top right; 36 middle left; 40 bottom left; 43 bottom all; 44 top right; 45 top left; 46; 47 bottom left;

48; 49 bottom right; 51 bottom left; 52 top; 54 bottom; 55 middle right and bottom left; 56 middle right and left; 58 bottom left and top right; 60 middle left; 61; 62
Leonard Hoffmann/SIL: Pp. 25 top right; 31 top right and bottom left; 32 bottom right; 33 top right; 53 top left, middle left and bottom left; 57 middle right;
Norman Larsen: P. 33 bottom right
James Marshall: P. 6 top left; P. 60 bottom right
Geoff McIlleron: Firefly Images: P 42 right
Ian Michler/SIL: P. 40 top right
Peter Pickford/SIL: Pp. 18 bottom; 21 top; 44 top left; 49 top left; 52 bottom left; 53 top right
Mike Picker: P. 30 Bottom right
Ariadne van Zandbergen/SIL: P. 55 top right
Hein von Horsten/SIL: Cover; P. 8 bottom
Clive Walker: P. 45 bottom right and left;
Alan Weaving: Pp. 9 top right; 35 middle left
(SIL: Struik Image Library)

BIBLIOGRAPHY
Abbott, C & Henning, S. 1984. *Southern African Butterflies*. Macmillan, Cape Town
Apps, P. 1992. *Wild Ways: Field Guide to Animal Behaviour*. Struik Publishers, Cape Town
Ginn, P J; McIlleron, W G & Milstein, P le S. 1989. *The Complete Book of Southern African Birds*. Struik Publishers, Cape Town
Holm, E & Scholtz, C H. 1985. *Insects of South Africa*. Butterworths Publishers, South Africa
Skinner, J D & Smithers, R H N. 1990. *The Mammals of the Southern African Subregion*. University of Pretoria, Pretoria
Stuart, C & T. 1994. *A Fieldguide to the Tracks and Signs of Southern and East African Wildlife*. Struik Publishers, Cape Town
Weaving, A. 2000. *Southern African Insects and their World*. Struik Publishers, Cape Town

GLOSSARY

Abdomen – The rear section of an insect, spider or crab body

Adaptation – A feature or pattern of growth that allows a plant or animal to live in a particular environment

Aerate – Process of adding air to the soil by digging

Aposematic coloration – Warning colours

Arboreal – Living in trees

Browser – An animal that feeds mainly off trees and shrubs

Camouflage – Colours or patterns on an animal that help to hide it by blending in with its background

Carcass – Animal remains

Cartilage – White, tough flexible tissue attached to the bones of animals

Carnivore – An animal that eats meat

Carrion – Dead rotting flesh of any animal

Clan – A large family that forms a close group

Colony – A group of animals living together

Debris – A collection of animal or vegetable matter

Decomposers – Animals or organisms that assist in breaking down vegetable and animal matter

Diurnal – Active during the day

Downwind – In the direction in which the wind is blowing

Endangered – A term applied to an animal that is threatened with extinction

Entrails – Internal organs, especially the intestines

Fertilize – A process by which pollen is introduced into the female part of a plant, or sperm introduced into the egg of a female, so that a new plant, or young animal, can develop

Fibrous – Made up of fibres, or thin strands

Forage – Search for food

Fungus (*pl.* **fungi**) – A plant without leaves or flowers that grows on other plants or decaying vegetation

Germinating – Sprouting of a new plant from a seed or from a spore

Grazer – An animal that feeds mainly on grass

Habitat – An animal's home, the area in which it lives

Herbivore – An animal that feeds on plants

Host – An animal or plant harbouring a parasite

Intestine – A long tube in an animal's body that helps digest food, and carries it from stomach to anus

Keratin – A tough fibrous substance (as in horns, nails, claws and hooves)

Larva (*pl.* **larvae**) – The young of an insect that hatches from an egg. It does not look like the adult. Caterpillars are butterfly larvae

Nymph – A young insect that looks like the adult, except that it has no wings

Maggots – Larvae, especially of flies

Mammal – A term for animals that are warm-blooded, have milk-producing glands, bear live young and are partly covered with hair

Mimic (**mimicry**) – To copy the appearance (or activities) of another species

Moult – A process by which animals shed feathers, hair or skin to allow for continued growth

Nocturnal – Active at night

Nomadic – Roaming from place to place

Omnivore – An animal that feeds on plants and animals

Parasite – An animal living in or on, and feeding on, another animal

Pheromone – A chemical released by an animal that is recognized by another of the same species

Poach (**poacher**) – To capture/kill animals illegally, usually to sell for commercial gain

Pollinate – A process by which pollen is transferred to the female part of a plant, so that a new plant can develop

Predator – An animal that catches and kills other animals for food

Prey – An animal that is killed by another for food

Raptor – Bird of prey

Retractable (of lions' claws) – Claws that can be withdrawn into a sheath until needed for capturing prey

Rhizomes – Underground roots

Scavenger – An animal that will eat almost any dead or even rotten food

Saliva – The liquid secreted by a gland in the mouth that helps with chewing and digestion

Species – A group of animals or plants with common characteristics, which breed only among themselves

Territory – An area defended by the occupant against others of its own kind

Vertebrae – Bones of the backbone